THE BATTLE INSIDE EVERY MAN
No More Excuses. No More Silence. It's Time To Rise

Blaise Tshibwabwa

Malachi Publications
Edmonton, Alberta, Canada

Published by:
Malachi Publications
Edmonton, Alberta, Canada
ISBN: 978-1-0693606-4-9

Cover design by: Blaise Tshibwabwa
For more information, contact: ejmialberta@gmail.com

Printed in Canada

DEDICATION

To every man in the cave… and to those who helped me find my voice there.

To every man who ever felt unseen,
who ever cried in silence,
who ever questioned if he was enough—
This book is for you.

You are not forgotten.
You are not disqualified.
There is power in your solitude.
There is purpose in your becoming.
And there is fire in your future.

To my wife, **Joelle (JL) Tshibwabwa** —thank you for your constant strength, your prayers, and your unwavering belief in the call of God on my life. You walk with me, war with me, and remind me who I am when I forget. You are my covering and my crown.

To my father, **Dr. Eli T. Tshibwabwa** —thank you for the example of hard work, quiet faith, and resilience. Your name carries weight, and I pray my life honors that weight well.

To my mother, **Rosalie Tshibwabwa** —thank you for your love, discipline, and the wisdom you planted early in me. You taught me how to read, how to believe, and how to pray. Your strength is part of my foundation, and I will forever honor it.
This one is for the brothers in the shadows.
It's time to rise.

— Blaise

ACKNOWLEDGMENTS

I want to thank the One who found me in the fire—Jesus Christ, the Author and Finisher of my faith. Every page of this book is a reflection of grace, forged through seasons of testing, silence, and surrender. I did not write from the mountaintop. I wrote from the cave, the valley, the furnace—and I found Him there.

To my wife, **Joelle (JL) Tshibwabwa**—thank you for standing beside me, believing with me, and praying through the pressure. You are more than a partner—you are strength, counsel, and beauty wrapped in fire. You saw the weight I carried and reminded me who I am.

To my father, **Dr. Eli T. Tshibwabwa**—your life has been a quiet sermon of sacrifice, hard work, and perseverance. Thank you for showing me what responsibility looks like in action.

To my mother, **Rosalie Tshibwabwa**—you taught me to read, to think, and to pray. Your early discipline-built pillars I still lean on. This book carries your imprint in every word.

To every brother who ever opened up, wept in silence, or asked the deeper questions—I hear you. You are not alone. And this book was written with you in mind.
To the **Encounter Jesus Ministries Alberta** family—thank you for allowing me to grow, stretch, fall, and rise again. Your prayers cover more than you know.

And finally, to every man who will pick up this book—whether by faith or by curiosity—I pray you see your own story in these pages and feel the hand of God pulling you up and through.

We rise through the fire. Not in spite of it, but because of it.

With honor,
—Blaise Tshibwabwa

ABOUT THE AUTHOR

Blaise Tshibwabwa is a passionate voice for spiritual transformation, identity, and purpose. A minister, author, and mentor to men and women across generations, he is known for blending depth with fire—offering bold truth wrapped in compassion and clarity.

Through *Encounter Jesus Ministries Alberta*, Blaise has helped many rediscover their calling, rebuild from brokenness, and rise into God's original design for their lives. His writing speaks especially to those navigating silent struggles—men who feel overlooked, pressured, or forgotten.

He is also the author of *How to Lead Spiritually as a Woman, 40 Days of Fire and Glory,* and *The Ultimate Guide to Starting a Business and Career.*

Blaise lives in Edmonton, Alberta with his wife **Joelle (JL)** and their children. Together, they serve their local and online communities with a heart for prayer, teaching, and spiritual renewal.
Follow and connect:
📖 YouTube Channel: @PrayerWithBlaise
✉ Email: ejmialberta@gmail.com

CHAPTER ONE
When Men Go Silent – The Hidden Fire in the Soul

There is a silence that is not peace. It is not rest. It is not the quiet of a man who has arrived—but the hush of one who is still fighting inside. Men don't always bleed in public. Sometimes, they bleed in worship. In waiting.

In wondering if they will ever become who God whispered they were.

This is the silence of Moses on the backside of the desert. The one who once thought he was ready. Now forgotten by Pharaoh. Forgotten by Israel. And perhaps, almost forgotten by himself. Yet in that wilderness silence, the fire did not die. It hid.

Deep in the soul of the man.
The truth is, some men carry fires they've never told anyone about. Prophetic burdens too heavy to name.

Dreams they buried in obedience. Questions they wrestled with under their breath. Their silence is not cowardice. It's consecration. It is the holy quiet of a man who has touched eternity but is still walking in time.

And when heaven wants to birth something new, it often starts with a man who has grown silent.

David was silent in the cave. Elijah, under the broom tree. Joseph, in the prison. Jesus, in the wilderness. This pattern is divine. God often answers the noise of a generation by setting apart a man in whom He plants a slow-burning flame. A man whose silence becomes the incubation chamber of divine fire.

You see, there are two kinds of silence. The silence of surrender—and the silence of gestation. One is defeat. The other is destiny. But to those around you, they may look the same.

The difference is in the fire.
A silent man with no fire is a man who has quit. But a silent man who carries fire is a threat to hell. Because one day, he will speak. And when he does, what he says will not be empty. It will be filled with weight. It will be marked by the time he spent hidden. And it will ignite others.

Men don't need more noise. They need altars. Sacred places to pour out what they carry, even when no one else is watching. They need moments with God that go beyond performance. Beyond applause. Beyond the mask of strength they've been forced to wear.

You have been quiet, not because you have nothing to say, but because God has not yet released the sound. The one who has been walking in fire, but hasn't had the words to explain it. The one who wakes up knowing there's more, but doesn't know how to reach it yet. Brother, your silence is not failure. It might be formation.

You are not lost. You are being found in fire. And when the time comes, your voice will not return empty. It will shake things. It will heal things. It will awaken things.

So wait. But don't go cold. Stay in the fire. Stay in the Word. Stay in posture.

Because when men go silent in God's presence, it's not the end. It's the beginning of a sound the earth has been waiting for.
Let the fire speak.

CHAPTER TWO
The Man Beneath the Armor – Silent Battles, Hidden Scars, and the Pressure to Be Enough

They see a man standing. Strong. Reliable. Holding it together. But they don't see the man beneath the armor.

The world teaches men how to perform, not how to process. From a young age, we are handed expectations like weapons: "Be strong." "Don't cry." "Figure it out." "Provide." "Lead." "Don't fail." But what they do not hand us is the oil for our wounds, or the grace for our confusion. We learn to wear armor before we learn to be healed. And so we walk—wounded warriors—succeeding externally while bleeding internally.

The pressure to be enough is a silent furnace. It burns without smoke. No applause greets a man's restraint. No camera captures the night he chose prayer over porn. No headlines tell of the day he resisted anger and chose to forgive. These things are not loud. But they are the real wars.

Goliath was not David's only battle. Before the giant, there were the bears. There were the lions. And before those, there were the nights. Alone. Rejected. Forgotten in the field. Many want the crown of David, but they forget that he was first invisible. Uninvited. Not even counted worthy to be introduced by his own father.

There are men reading this now who have never been properly seen. Not by their father. Not by their pastor. Not by their wife. They walk among crowds but feel unknown. They laugh, but it does not reach their soul. They carry burdens they cannot explain. Because to explain them would mean admitting that the armor is heavy, and the soul is tired.

And yet—God sees the man beneath the armor.
It was not the sword of Saul that made David a king. It was the tears. The nights of worship in the cave. The broken psalms he sang while fleeing for his life. It was what he carried in his spirit that qualified him—not what he wore on his body. His greatness was not in his victories. It was in his valleys.

The kingdom of God is built by men who have lost something. Men who have cried. Men who were not picked first, but were chosen by God anyway. Men who have scars not seen by flesh, but known in the spirit. You must understand this: the battles you fight in secret are often the battles that birth your authority in public.

Jacob became Israel not on a battlefield, but in a wrestling match—alone, under the stars. He wrestled not with a man, but with his past. With his fear. With his identity. With the ghost of who he had been and the demand of who he must become. And when God touched him, He did not strengthen Jacob's muscle—

He dislocated it. God gave him a limp that would preach for generations.

Because sometimes, the evidence that God has touched a man is not that he walks straight—but that he walks differently.

The pressure to be a man is real. But it is also a lie when it's divorced from grace. You were not called to impress people. You were not built to wear the mask forever. There is a man beneath the armor that God is after—the one you hide even from yourself. The one who wonders if he's still enough. The one who fears failing his children. The one who carries the disappointment of not being where he thought he'd be by now.

Let me say this plainly: God is not intimidated by the real you. He does not anoint the man you pretend to be. He touches the man who dares to bring his weakness, his questions, and his fatigue to the altar. Because only what is exposed can be healed. And only what is surrendered can be transformed.

The sword of Goliath was not forged for David—but it became his weapon. There are victories in your future that will come from the very thing that tried to kill you. There is purpose hidden in your pain. There is fire being born in the silence. But you must stop hiding. You must come out from behind the armor.

There is a generation of men waiting to see one man stand up in truth. Not just in strength—but in vulnerability. Not just in performance—but in presence. The world has enough actors. What it needs are altars. Men who become altars. Men who are not afraid to burn if it means others can live.
And maybe that's you.

Maybe your greatest battle is not with porn or money or fear—but with the lie that you are only valuable if you succeed. That you must always be the provider, the protector, the performer. But what if I told you that your Father in heaven never asked you to be the hero—He asked you to be the son?

Even Jesus, the Son of God, wore no armor. He wept. He rested. He listened. And when the pressure was greatest in Gethsemane—He bled from His face before He bled from His side. He showed us that even the perfect man must sometimes fall to His knees before He can stand on the cross.

And you, my brother, are no different. The man beneath the armor is the one God wants to use.
So take off the weight. The fake smile. The unspoken trauma. The fear of not being enough. Lay it down. And rise—not as the man people expect, but as the man heaven has chosen.

Because the world needs him. And heaven is waiting.

CHAPTER THREE
**The Battle for Identity – Between the Voice of God
and the Lies of Blood**

A man's identity is not first tested in the crowd. It is
tested in the silence after someone he trusted speaks a
lie over him.

And he believes it.

This is not about success. It is about the fracture before
the success. The contradiction in the soul of a man who
hears God calling but still remembers the voice of his
father saying, "You'll never be enough." The tension
between what was declared over you in heaven, and
what was whispered about you on earth.
Identity is not discovered casually.

It is wrestled for. And it is often fought in a place
where your bloodline and your spiritual lineage collide.
There is the blood of your family, yes, but there is the
blood of Christ. One speaks of patterns. The other
speaks of purpose. One pulls you back into the failures
of your father. The other calls you forward into the
image of the Son.

You must choose whose blood speaks louder.
The voice of God is clear: *"This is my beloved Son, in
whom I am well pleased."* But before Jesus ever
performed one miracle, He was baptized into identity.

Not function. Not gifting. Identity. And immediately after that affirmation, the Spirit led Him into the wilderness, not to enjoy identity, but to have it challenged. *"If you are the Son of God…"* That was the attack.

Satan didn't say "if you're powerful." He said, "If you're a son." Because the war has always been about identity. Not talent. Not titles. Identity. Because if a man knows who he is, he will never sell his birthright for applause, a woman's body, or a counterfeit crown.

But if he forgets who he is, he will wear any armor that feels accepted.

There are men right now who have become strangers to themselves. You do what you're expected to do. You say what they trained you to say. You shake hands. You work hard. You attend church. But beneath it, your soul is not at peace. Because you're living someone else's version of manhood, not heaven's blueprint.

The voice of God is gentle, but relentless. It comes not to flatter, but to name. And when God names a man, He delivers him from every false label placed by man.

Gideon was threshing wheat in fear when the angel said, *"Mighty man of valor."* But there was no army. No fame. Just fear. Confusion. Survival. And yet heaven's voice interrupted earth's history and declared something deeper. Gideon's family didn't see a warrior. His surroundings didn't affirm a leader. But the voice of God broke into the dust and called out what no one else could see.

This is the prophetic confrontation of identity: God speaks to your future while your past still has receipts. And you must decide whether to live by the memory of failure—or by the prophecy of who you are becoming.

Too many men have inherited pain and called it personality. You were told, "You're just like your uncle." "You have your father's temper." "You'll never change." These are bloodline lies. Familiar spirits speaking through familiar people. They tattoo shame into your soul until you forget you were made in the image of a God who creates, redeems, and restores.

You are not your dysfunction. You are not your addiction. You are not your broken marriage, your hidden struggle, or your family's curse. You are not your failures. You are not your absences. You are not your past.

You are who God says you are.
But that truth is not passive. It is prophetic. And it must be violently defended.

Elijah stood alone on Mount Carmel because he knew who he was. There were 850 prophets. One man. One

altar. One God. And fire came down not because Elijah had a crowd, but because he had clarity. When you know who you are, you stop begging for platforms. You stop copying other men. You stop posturing to be accepted. Because you're not performing—you're walking in revelation.
And revelation is the only antidote to generational confusion.

Moses was called to lead a nation, but his identity war raged between two worlds. He was raised as Egyptian royalty, but born as a Hebrew slave. One part of him was polished by Pharaoh's palace. The other part of him bled for his people. And in that split, Moses fled. He ran to the desert—not because he lacked calling, but because he lacked clarity.

There are men in deserts today not because they are lost, but because they are running from the conflict between two identities. One crafted by blood. One forged by fire. And until the burning bush speaks— until the divine voice interrupts the narrative—they live in hiding.

But God is not finished with you.
The voice of God does not only affirm. It awakens.

It interrupts. It renames. *Jacob became Israel. Saul became Paul. Simon became Peter.* And maybe today is the day you become who you really are. Not the man your bloodline made—but the man the blood of Jesus redeemed.

Because when your identity is revealed, your authority is released.

It is time to renounce the lies of blood. The curses spoken by broken fathers. The insecurity passed down through silent homes and absent men. The addiction that stalks your bloodline like a shadow.

It is time to tear down the altars of false identity and raise up the name that God has called you by.

"You are my son."
"You are chosen."
"You are a priest and a king."
"You are mine."

Let the voice of the Father be louder than the failures of your lineage. Let the fire of revelation burn away every mask. Let this be the chapter that breaks the spell of performance, and awakens the truth that you were not just born—you were sent.

And if you were sent, then you are not random. You are not a mistake. You are not forgotten. You are a man on assignment. And your identity is the weapon that hell fears the most.

So rise. And become.

CHAPTER FOUR
He Walked With God – Enoch and the Mystery of Masculine Presence

There are men whose power is not in their voice—but in their walk.

Not because they are famous. But because they are known… in heaven.

Enoch walked with God. That's all the Bible says. No titles. No armies. No dramatic miracles. Just one thing: *he walked with God.* And that one phrase is enough to rewrite what we think manhood is.

He did not build temples. He did not slay giants. He simply stayed in step with the Creator. And heaven could not bear the distance. So God took him.

Not because he was loud. But because he was close. We have raised a generation of men who know how to build, lead, preach, and perform—but who have forgotten how to walk. We have exchanged presence for performance. Depth for display. And now our homes, churches, and souls are heavy with movement—but empty of presence.

The strength of a man is not found in how many people he can lead. It is found in how closely he walks with the God who leads him.
Enoch was not defined by his accomplishments—but by his alignment. He lived in rhythm with the invisible. He moved in cadence with the Eternal. And because of that, he carried something that our generation is starving for: spiritual presence.

Not the kind that shouts. The kind that shakes.
There is a holy weight that follows a man who walks with God. He may not say much. But when he enters a room, the atmosphere bends. He may not boast. But when he lays hands on his children, something eternal is transferred. He may not have a platform. But when he kneels, heaven records it.

We've made masculinity a contest of who can do the most. But real masculinity begins with who abides the deepest.

Adam walked with God in the cool of the day. Until sin interrupted that rhythm. Enoch picked up that lost frequency and restored it—one step at a time. He showed us that presence is not just a Sunday event. It's a lifestyle. A posture. A path.

And the truth is: every man is walking somewhere. The only question is—are you walking with God?

We walk with our ambitions. Our pain. Our guilt. Our memories. We walk with the opinions of people. With the pressure to succeed. With the fear of being seen as weak. But few walk with God. Few live like His presence is oxygen. Few carry their masculinity with such reverence that every decision is filtered through communion.

The man who walks with God does not need to prove himself. His authority comes from proximity. His stability comes from intimacy. His power is not borrowed—it is birthed. It is formed in the silent places, where ego dies and sonship is born.
And this… is what many men are missing.

Not advice. Not motivation. Presence.

We are addicted to noise but allergic to stillness. We are trained to conquer, but not to commune. We think strength is in our output. But real strength begins in outpouring. Before God uses a man to shape nations, He first teaches that man how to sit… still… with Him.

Enoch did not disappear because he was extraordinary. He disappeared because he had become fully aligned. God said, in essence, "You're already walking this closely with Me—come home."
There is something terrifying and beautiful about that. Terrifying, because it exposes how distant most of us

live from the Spirit. Beautiful, because it means we can return.

We can return to the walk.
You do not need a new anointing. You need a new alignment. You don't need louder prayers. You need longer silence. You don't need to become more impressive. You need to become more present.
Because when a man walks with God, he becomes a gateway. His life becomes an altar. His footsteps carry fire. He stops reacting—and starts discerning.

He doesn't chase moments—he carries atmospheres. And that man is not forgotten when he leaves. Because he leaves a trail of presence behind him.
This is the mystery of Enoch. The masculine mystery the Church has neglected. The truth we lost in our race for relevance.

God is calling for men who will walk again. Men who will say, "I don't just want to work for You—I want to walk with You."
And maybe that's you.

Maybe your strength isn't in doing more. Maybe it's in slowing down until your feet are walking the same path as His. Maybe your power won't come from a new opportunity—but from returning to the place where His presence makes you whole.

You don't need to be faster.
You don't need to be busier.
You need to walk.

For in walking, you become known.
And when heaven knows your walk, earth cannot
ignore your presence.
Enoch walked with God.
And he was not… for God took him.
What a way to live.
What a way to leave.

CHAPTER FIVE
**The Wound That Teaches – Jacob's Limp and the
Men Who Wrestle**

There are some lessons a man can only learn in the
dark.

Not in a classroom and not in a sermon. But in a
moment when he is finally alone and stripped of image,
titles, excuses, and noise. A moment when God doesn't
come to comfort him… but to confront him.

Jacob had spent most of his life getting ahead. Jacob
learned early how to survive. Jacob knew how to reach
for what he wanted, even if it meant deceiving someone
to get it. However, Jacob was not wicked. Jacob was
just shaped by a world that taught him to fight for
everything and trust no one. Especially not God.

And yet, God still had amazing plans for him.
Jacob was not without blessing. He had wealth; Wives;
Children and Servants. A future. But something was
still missing. Something no one could give him. Not
even the birthright he stole.

Jacob had a future, but he had no solid foundation. He
had lots of things, but no peace. He had motion, but no
name that fit who he was becoming.
And God would not let him build legacy on broken
identity.

So one night, it happened.
He sent everyone ahead. He was alone by the river. No
more props. No more people. No more running. And
into that silence, God came—not gently, but as a Man
who wrestled him to the ground.

Jacob didn't recognize it at first. This wasn't a thief or a
threat. It was something holy. But the holiness did not
come with softness. It came in the form of resistance.

Because sometimes, God will fight the man you
pretend to be… to reveal the man He created you to be.

Jacob fought. All night. Not with fists, but with
identity. Not with muscles, but with memory. The
wounds of his past. The fear of his future. The ache of
feeling like he had to earn what should have been freely
spoken: "You are loved. You are chosen. You are
enough."

But those words had never come. So Jacob became a
fighter. A grasper. A builder. But not yet a son.
And that night, he held onto God with everything he
had. Not because he understood what was happening—
but because something in him knew: "I can't leave this
night the same."

The wound came just before the breakthrough.
God touched Jacob's hip and dislocated it. Not to
punish him—but to mark him. To say, "You will never

walk like you used to. Not because you are weak—but because you have seen Me and lived."
The limp was not a curse. It was a prophecy.

Because the men God uses most deeply… are often the ones He wounds most personally.

Jacob could no longer run. No longer pretend. No longer stand tall in his own strength. He had to lean. He had to limp. He had to depend. And that's when the question came.

"What is your name?"
It was never really about his name. It was about his truth. For the first time, Jacob had to say it out loud. No games. No deflection. No mask.

"I am Jacob."

That confession broke something open in heaven. And God said, "No more. That name belonged to the man who ran. The man who tricked. The man who never believed he was enough. But you… you have wrestled. You have held on. You have survived the night. You shall now be called Israel." And just like that—Jacob was renamed by the God he fought.

This is how real change comes to a man. Not through titles. Not through performance. But through presence.

Through honesty. Through wrestling when it would be easier to quit.
Some of the men reading this know exactly what that night feels like.

You've been wrestling silently. With questions. With guilt. With shame. With the fear that you're not who people think you are. With the pressure to lead, but the feeling of being lost. And maybe no one sees it. But heaven does.

And God has not come to crush you. He's come to confront you. To hold you in a divine wrestle until the image cracks… and the real you stands up.
You do not have to keep pretending.

Let the limp speak. Let it teach your sons that God can be trusted in the dark. Let it remind your soul that power is not in your perfection—it's in your surrender.

You are not Jacob anymore. That name was for the fight. But you are becoming Israel now. A man who wrestled and did not let go. A man who walks differently—not because he's less—but because he's finally aligned.

The wound didn't destroy you.
It made you walk like a man who's been with God.
And that's the walk the world is waiting for.

CHAPTER SIX
Men at the Altar – Why Real Strength Begins in the Spirit

There is a place where men are no longer measured by muscle, money, or mastery—but by fire. And that place is the altar.

Not the stage. Not the boardroom. Not the gym.
The ALTAR.

Before God gives a man a platform, He invites him to a posture. Before He makes a man a leader, He makes him a priest. And before He allows you to influence others, He tests what you burn in private. Because strength is not proven in how loud a man can shout— it's proven in how low he can kneel.

We have built a culture that tells men to be powerful, but not prayerful. To be successful, but not surrendered. To conquer the world, but ignore the altar. And now we are raising men who can build empires but can't lead their homes. Men who know how to take charge—but don't know how to stay still in the presence of God.

But every real man of God—every one Heaven trusts— was built at the altar.

The altar is not a place of performance. It is a place of death. It is where ego dies. Pride breaks. Masks fall.

And the man you've been pretending to be gets
exposed by the God who already sees you.

The altar is where Moses' staff became more than
wood—it became a weapon. It is where Elijah called
down fire, not because of charisma, but because his
heart was aligned. It is where Abraham laid down the
very thing he loved most—not because he was weak,
but because he was ready.

You do not know how strong a man is until you see
what he's willing to lay down.

The altar is not popular. It will never trend. It will never
feel impressive. Because it is not about being seen—it
is about being transformed. This is the place where men
become more than what culture calls them. They
become what heaven needs them to be: priests, fathers,
watchmen, sons.

We live in a world full of men with influence but no
incense. Men who have image, but no oil. But the
kingdom of God doesn't run on image. It runs on fire.
And fire only falls where something has died.
This is why the altar is the birthplace of true strength.
Because it's the only place where the Holy Spirit can
burn away the lesser man so the real man can rise.

You cannot outsource this. You cannot fake this. You
cannot substitute altar time with religious activity. Real

strength begins in the spirit. In prayer. In tears. In worship that no one sees. In conversations with God that have nothing to do with asking—but everything to do with becoming.

And if you have never wept on your knees, you don't yet know your full weight.
If you have never laid your titles, your plans, your timelines, your wounds on the altar—you are still leading in your own strength.
But there is another way.

There is a way of fire. A way of presence. A way of masculine priesthood that does not begin with performance, but with posture. It does not begin with movement, but with stillness. It is what Jesus modeled. The Son of God, the Lion of Judah, knelt in Gethsemane before He stood at Calvary.

He prayed until blood came from His face.
And then… He rose.

Real men pray. Real men worship. Real men build altars in secret, because they know public power is useless without private presence.

And maybe this is your call to return.

Not to more ministry. But to the presence. Not to more leadership techniques. But to the fire. Not to another

event or another appearance. But to the place where
God waits—not for your strength, but for your
surrender.
You are not too busy. You are not too far gone. You are
not too broken. The altar doesn't ask you to come
clean. It asks you to come open.

Because what dies on the altar doesn't stay dead.
It becomes fire. So come again.

Come not as a warrior, but as a son. Come not to
impress, but to be changed. Come not to bring a sermon
or a strategy—but to bring your heart.
And when you do… He will meet you there.
And the man who rises will not be the man who knelt.

CHAPTER SEVEN
The Seed and the Sword – Building, Fathering, and Fighting

Every man is entrusted with two things from heaven: a seed to plant… and a sword to protect.
One brings life. The other defends it. One speaks to vision. The other to warfare. And the man who does not understand both will fail at legacy. Because building without defending is blindness. And defending without building is exhaustion. But when a man knows how to build and how to fight—he becomes dangerous to darkness and fruitful for generations.

The first thing God gave Adam was not a pulpit—it was a garden. A territory. A seed to steward. Something to name. Something to multiply. Something that could grow under his watch. This is the masculine mandate: build something with your life that heaven can bless. But seeds are fragile.

They don't scream. They don't fight back. They don't announce their potential. They just sit there—quiet, buried, and full of promise. And it is the man's role to protect them. To water them. To shield them from winds, wild beasts, and weeds. It is not glamorous work. But it is sacred.

You are a man because God trusted you with something small that can become something great—if you refuse to abandon it.
Your marriage is a seed. Your children are seeds.
Your business is a seed. Your purity is a seed. Your time with God is a seed. Your words—yes, even your silence—are planting something.

The question is: are you watching over what you planted?

Because just as God gave Adam a seed, He gave him a sword. He said, "Guard it." That means there is an enemy. That means there are forces that want to spoil what you've been called to build. It means you cannot afford to be passive. Not with your mind. Not with your household. Not with your altar.

The serpent did not come for Adam's strength. He came for his silence. And when Adam failed to speak, to stand, to fight—he lost his ground. Not because he was weak. But because he was absent.

The world is not being destroyed by weak men. It is being hollowed out by distracted ones. Men who are present in body, but missing in spirit. Men who can make money, but can't lay hands. Men who can raise a brand, but not a child. Men who show up in church, but never show up at the altar. But God is restoring warrior-builders again.

Not perfect men. Present ones. Not loud men. Altar
men. Not violent men. Vision men. Men who hear from
God, fight for their families, and carry a builder's spirit
and a priest's fire. Men who understand the balance
between tenderness and tenacity. Between presence and
protection.

You are that man. You are not called to just survive.
You are called to plant, to guard, and to multiply. You
are called to lay foundations with your hands and raise
altars with your tears. You are called to teach your sons
how to love and teach your enemies why you're not
afraid.

And you must carry both tools at once.
There are moments to dig deep. And moments to draw
your sword. There are days when the Lord will give
you rest. And there are days when He will hand you a
fight. Do not be shocked when opposition comes—it is
proof that your seed matters.

You are not under attack because you are weak. You
are under attack because what you carry is prophetic.
The devil doesn't waste time on men with empty hands.
He targets builders. He targets carriers. He targets
fathers. He targets men who have planted something
worth stealing. But your fight is not just for you.

It is for your house. Your city. Your name. Your children's children. You are not just defending a season—you are defending a legacy. So don't put down your sword. And don't neglect your seed.
This is your mandate: build… and fight.
And if you do, the generations behind you will not just inherit land. They will inherit your fire.

CHAPTER EIGHT
When the Mantle Falls – Sons, Mentors, and Spiritual Legacy

Every man leaves something behind.
Not just money. Not just property. But spirit. Presence.
Example. And the question is never *if* a man will leave
a legacy—it's *what kind* of legacy he will leave behind.
You can leave memories or mantles. Silence or
instruction. Wounds or wisdom.
But you will leave something.

Elijah stood at the edge of heaven and earth with fire
still in his bones. His journey was not just about the
miracles he had done. It was about the mantle he would
release. Because true greatness is not proven in how
high you rise—but in what still burns when you're
gone.

A mantle is not a metaphor. It is a spiritual trust. A
weight of authority, intimacy, and function in the Spirit
that can be transferred, but never faked. And when
Elijah was taken up, he did not give Elisha fame—he
gave him fire.

But Elisha didn't receive the mantle by standing
casually at a distance. He followed closely. He stayed
when others left. He asked boldly. He was present in
moments of transition. And that's what sons do. They

don't just admire. They carry. They catch. They continue.
We are living in a generation of gifted men, but very few carry legacy.

We have built crowds but not fathers. We have leaders who protect their platforms, but do not pour into sons. We have churches full of men who are talented, but untethered. And we wonder why mantles disappear. We wonder why generations repeat the same dysfunctions. We wonder why movements die when a man dies.

The answer is simple: no sons. No transfer.
And without transfer, we start from scratch. Again. And again. And again.

This is not how heaven operates. God builds through continuity. Abraham to Isaac. Isaac to Jacob. Moses to Joshua. Elijah to Elisha. Paul to Timothy. Jesus to the twelve. Men who knew that what they carried must outlive them—or it was never legacy in the first place.

There is a mantle on your life. You may not feel it. You may not think it's significant. But if you are a man of the Spirit, then you are a carrier of something sacred. And that sacred thing must be passed on.

You must live in such a way that your ceiling becomes someone else's floor. That your pain becomes someone else's wisdom. That your scars become someone else's map. That your fire becomes someone else's inheritance. You were not called to just survive. You were called to multiply. But that cannot happen if you don't open your life. If you don't take sons. If you don't humble yourself and pour into someone who may never thank you publicly, but who will carry what you gave him privately.

Legacy is not built on applause. It's built in obscurity. In prayer. In meals. In conversations. In sacrifice. In time. It is not loud. But it is eternal.
We are called to be both Elisha and Elijah.

You must be humble enough to follow—and bold enough to pass on. You must pursue wisdom with fire—and release wisdom with love. You must never hoard what heaven gave you. The mantle must fall. And when it does, someone must be close enough to catch it.

Fathers—look for sons. Sons—stay close to fire. Mentors—pour. Students—listen. Men—invest in someone who is not you. Because the day will come when the chariots of fire arrive. And you won't get to plan the timing.

You won't get to delay the moment. You won't get to hold the mantle forever. But you *can* decide where it lands.

Live with that in mind. Pray with that in mind. Lead with that in mind.
And when your time comes, may you not be remembered for what you built—but for who you raised. May the mantle fall—and may fire live on.

CHAPTER NINE
Deliver Us From Ourselves – Lust, Power, and the Fall of Kings

The most dangerous WAR a man will ever fight is the one inside him.

Not war against demons! Not war against people! But against himself, his impulses, his appetites, his secrets. The parts of him that no one sees. The rooms in his soul where light has never entered. It is possible to defeat external enemies and still be ruined by what you never conquered privately.

Ask Samson.
Ask David.
Ask Solomon.

It is not the absence of calling that destroys kings—it is the absence of restraint.

Samson had strength. David had a heart after God. Solomon had wisdom beyond his years. But all three fell—not because they didn't know God, but because they refused to surrender one part of their soul.

They gave God everything except their appetite. Everything except their silence. Everything except the room where lust hides and power whispers. And it cost them everything.

There is a place in every man's soul where the battle is not about right or wrong—but about lordship. A place where God is either everything, or just an accessory to your ambitions. Lust does not begin in the eyes—it begins in the soul. In loneliness. In entitlement. In the craving to feel alive when something deeper is dying.

The fall of a man rarely starts with an action. It starts with a slow drift from the altar. It starts when prayer becomes routine. When worship becomes performance. When secrets become tolerable. When no one holds you accountable because everyone sees you as strong. But being seen as strong is not the same as being safe.

There are men right now—gifted, respected, even anointed—who are falling quietly. Their hands still lift in church. Their voices still echo with Scripture. But their hearts are leaking. Their fire is fading. Their oil is contaminated. And hell is not afraid of what they say publicly—it is feeding on what they excuse privately.

Lust is not just sexual. Lust is any hunger that replaces God.

It is a need for attention. A thirst for power. A longing to be touched, seen, noticed—without the willingness to be truly healed. And when these cravings are ignored, they grow roots. Roots that bypass your performance and choke your soul in places sermons

can't reach. And one day… the cracks give way. And the fall is loud.

David's fall began long before Bathsheba. It began when he stopped going to war. When he stayed behind. When he got comfortable. When the weight of kingship felt like enough—and intimacy with God became secondary. He looked. He lingered. He took. He covered. He murdered. And the man who had slain Goliath… couldn't slay his own desire.
Because a man who doesn't confront his appetites will eventually feed them—even if it kills everything he built.

You don't need deliverance from people. You need deliverance from the man in the mirror.
You need to be rescued from the excuses. From the patterns. From the cycles you've normalized. From the moments you say, "It's not that bad." From the flesh that says, "I deserve this." From the inner voice that justifies sin because you're tired, broken, or successful.

But you were not made to be a cautionary tale.
You were made to finish well.

The Spirit of God is still stronger than your flesh. The cross is still enough. The blood still delivers. The fire still cleanses. But it cannot heal what you continue to hide. And it cannot save what you still want more than you want freedom.

You must choose. Not just once—but daily.
Die to the part of you that lusts for escape. Kill the
fantasy. Confront the conversation. Block the number.
Get rid of the image. Destroy the idol. Ask for help. Let
the fire of conviction burn deeper than your desire for
pleasure. Because pleasure fades. But legacy speaks.

This chapter is not written to condemn you.
It's written to call you out.

You are better than what you're entertaining.
You are stronger than what you keep returning to.
You are a king. A priest. A son. A watchman.
So act like it. Live like it. Pray like it. And if you've
fallen—get up.

There is still time to be healed. To be pure. To be
whole. To be the man your children can admire. To be
the husband who can be trusted. To be the leader who
doesn't have to fake strength—but carries fire in his
bones because he finally surrendered fully.

Deliver us from ourselves, Lord.
From the small compromises.
From the justifications.
From the fantasy.
From the pride.
From the silence.

Let us not be men who carried revelation but lacked repentance. Let us not be kings who sat on thrones but lost the presence. Let us not fall… because we refused to be honest.

Deliver us.
Rescue us.
Restore us.
And may our stories be fire—not failure.

CHAPTER TEN
The Watchman's Warning – A Prophetic Voice in a Perverse Generation

There are men who are called to see what others ignore. Men who are awake when others sleep. Men who carry a weight not because they asked for it, but because heaven assigned it. These are the watchmen.

They are not celebrities. They are not influencers. They are not always found in the spotlight. But when a nation begins to drift, God looks for them. When a generation begins to fall asleep at the wheel, God raises them up. Their eyes are open. Their ears are trained. Their words are fire.

Not because they want to be loud. But because they refuse to be silent.

The world is not just changing—it is unraveling. Truth is no longer treasured. Holiness is mocked. God is treated like a myth. And evil no longer hides. It parades. It dares. It flaunts. And while this generation scrolls and celebrates itself into numbness, heaven is still asking the same question it asked Ezekiel: *"Son of man, can these bones live?"*

The role of the watchman is not comfortable. It is confrontational. It is prophetic. It is costly.

Because to be a watchman is to be pierced by what you see. It is to carry God's burden for a people who no longer fear Him. It is to weep over altars that are broken, and cry out for homes that are spiritually vacant. It is to hear footsteps in the Spirit before the storm arrives.

You feel it, don't you?
Something is off. Something is shifting. The headlines say progress, but your spirit says deception. The world calls it freedom, but your discernment calls it rebellion. And while the Church argues about trends and style, the foundations are cracking.

And yet… so many men stay quiet.
We were not born to be passive. We were not designed to be polite when eternity is at stake.
You were made to speak. To sound the alarm. To pray like fire and preach like thunder. To love boldly and warn fiercely. You are a watchman.
And if you don't sound the trumpet, the blood is on your hands.

God is not looking for perfect men. He is looking for present ones. Alert ones. Ones who have seen the danger approaching and refuse to look away.
He is looking for men who are not afraid to call sin what it is, to call their brothers back to the altar, to cry out over their cities, and to weep between the porch and the altar. The prophet is not here to blend in. The

watchman is not here to entertain. He is here to interrupt.

Your voice may not be welcome. But it is needed. Your burden may be heavy. But it is holy.

Because watchmen carry fire in their bones. They are awake when culture sleeps. They are grieved when others laugh. They are stretched between heaven and earth. And they do not just see the enemy—they sound the alarm.

You don't need to be a pastor to carry this call. You just need to be a man who is done with silence. A man who will not allow the devil to walk through his home, his church, or his city without resistance. A man who refuses to go numb while the gates are burning.

This generation is perverse—but not beyond redemption. And God is still searching for men who will stand on the wall and say, "Not on my watch." Men who pray at midnight. Men who fast when no one sees. Men who raise holy children. Men who fight in the Spirit. Men who speak the Word of God with fire and tears.

This is not the hour to retreat. It is the hour to cry loud and spare not.

You are not too young. You are not too unqualified.
You are not too late. You are not too broken.
God is still assigning watchmen. So if your spirit has
been restless, if your dreams have been stirring, if your
eyes have been open while others scroll—take it as
your call. The trumpet is in your hand now. Blow it.

CHAPTER ELEVEN
Rise as Flame – Becoming the Man Nations and Families Need

There are moments in history when heaven doesn't just speak—it sends men. Not just men with opinions.

But men with fire.

Not fire that comes from microphones or followers. But fire that comes from the altar.

Every generation carries crisis. But not every generation produces men who carry answers. Men who stand between what is… and what could be. Men who don't just fit into the culture—but confront it. Not with rage, but with righteousness. Not with volume, but with vision. Not with pride, but with presence.

The world does not need another influencer. It needs a flame.

It needs men who have been set ablaze in the secret place. Men who pray with scars. Who father with oil. Who build with tears. Who do not chase trends, but host truth. Men whose lives preach louder than their voices. Men who are not safe—but surrendered.
You were not born just to pay bills and behave. You were born to carry fire into a cold world.

That fire doesn't come from ambition. It comes from brokenness surrendered at the feet of God. It comes from the cave, from the altar, from the midnight cry. And when it ignites, it changes everything. It makes you impossible to ignore. Because real fire doesn't ask for attention. It demands it.

Moses came down from the mountain with fire in his face.

Elijah called it down until it swallowed the altar. John the Baptist carried it in his voice. Jesus carried it in His eyes.

The early church carried it in their bones. And now—God wants to put it in you.

This world is not falling apart because darkness is strong.

It's falling apart because men are dim. Because fathers are absent. Because leaders have grown soft. Because purity has become a punchline. Because the altar has been replaced by algorithms. But fire is coming again.

And it will not fall randomly. It will fall on men who have made themselves available. Men who say, "Here I am. Light me up. Burn through me. I will be Your voice in this generation." This is not romantic. It is violent.

Because when you carry fire, you become a threat. A disruption. A target. Hell marks you. But so does heaven. And once heaven marks you, nothing on earth can own you. Not lust. Not fear. Not the past. Not culture. Not shame. Not failure. You become flame.

And flame doesn't negotiate. It doesn't bow. It doesn't blend. It burns. Your wife needs that flame. Your children need that flame. Your church needs that flame. Your community needs that flame. Your own heart needs to see you rise—finally, as the man you were born to be.

Not half-awake. Not half-surrendered. Not half-believing.

But fully alive. Fully submitted. Fully on fire. Because when a man becomes flame, he becomes dangerous to hell and healing to everyone else. He becomes clarity in confusion. Order in chaos. Light in the shadow. A voice crying in the wilderness, "Prepare the way of the Lord!"

You are not too broken to carry this. You are not too late. You are not too small. You are not too old. You are not too sinful. But you must rise.
Not by willpower. But by surrender. Not by hype. But by holiness. Not by trying harder. But by yielding deeper.

The nations are not waiting for perfection. They're waiting for fire. The families are not asking for performance. They're asking for presence. And heaven is not recruiting celebrities. It is commissioning flames.

Let that be you.

Let your life burn so brightly that others find their way back to God through your obedience. Let your purity silence shame. Let your words carry weight. Let your actions provoke hunger. Let your leadership open heaven over your home.

Rise as flame. And do not apologize for the fire.

CHAPTER TWELVE
The Final Call – The Sound of Men Marching Home

There is a sound rising in the spirit. It is not the sound of applause. Not the sound of entertainment. Not the sound of opinion or trend. It is the sound of men… marching home.

Men who have wandered are returning. Men who have fallen are standing again. Men who have survived fire are stepping out of the ashes. Men who were hidden are coming forth. Not just to attend church—but to become the Church.

This is the final call.
The call for men to wake up from compromise. To break free from cycles. To silence the shame. To stop waiting for perfect conditions, and step fully into the war they were born for.

You can feel it, can't you? The world is shifting. The shadows are growing bolder. The lines are being drawn. And heaven is not asking for crowds. Heaven is looking for *consecrated men*. Men who do not need to be begged. Men who do not need to be entertained. Men who have heard the call—and answered with their lives.

This is that moment.

The moment when you stop asking, *"God, are You going to use me?"*

And start declaring, *"Here I am. Send me."*
You've carried the pain. You've fought the inner war. You've stood through the fire. You've limped with grace. You've been refined, confronted, corrected, and called. And now the trumpet sounds—not to tell you to rest—but to tell you it's time.

Time to lead. Time to fight. Time to speak. Time to build.

Time to walk as if the presence of God lives inside you—because it does.

This world does not need more noise. It needs more presence. It needs more men whose lives echo eternity. Men who have seen too much to be casual. Men who have been forgiven too deeply to live small. Men who have found joy too real to stay silent.

You are not a mistake. You are not a burden. You are not forgotten. You are not finished.

You are being summoned.

Back to the ALTAR. Back to the WORD. Back to your HOUSE. Back to your ASSIGNMENT. Back to the

PLACE WHERE FIRE FELL AND THE VOICE OF GOD THUNDERED.

You don't need another sermon. You need to obey the last whisper. You don't need another confirmation. You need to get up and move. Because this isn't about how you started.

It's about how you finish.

You are being called into a march. Not of men who are perfect—but of men who are purified. A company of fathers, sons, leaders, warriors, servants, prophets, mentors, builders. They are not loud in the streets. But they are mighty in the Spirit.
They are returning home. To righteousness. To responsibility.

To restoration. To legacy. To the Father.
This is not just your final chapter. It is your first commissioning.

Let the devil see you rise. Let your family hear your voice. Let the heavens witness a man who made it out. Let the fire return to your eyes. Let the sound of your footsteps tell hell, *"You should've killed me when you had the chance."*

You are not just walking. You are marching. And the sound of your life will echo across generations—

because you didn't just survive. You didn't just learn. **You answered.**
The final call has gone out. And the men are marching home.

The Return of the Burning Man

He does not walk like the others. He does not speak to impress. He does not seek applause or approval.

This man, has seen too much. Heard too much. Bled too much. He is not just a man. He is a signal. A remnant. He is a witness.

HE IS THE BURNING MAN.

Hell hoped that he would quit. Culture hoped that he would compromise. Religion hoped that he would stay quiet. But the fire in his bones said NO. The voice of the Lord kept calling. The mantle would not lift. The altar would not die. And the oil began to flow again!

This is the hour of return.
Not to normal. To fire. Not to tradition.
But, To truth.

Not to performance. But To power.
The world is not waiting for more men with answers. It is waiting for men who have *been with God.*

Men whose shadows carry healing. Men whose tears are intercession. Men whose silence is authority. Men whose very presence makes demons tremble and generations hope again.

This is the return of the burning man. The priest. The father. The flame. The one who has chosen the altar over the platform. Holiness over applause.
Obedience over opinion. Presence over personality.
Fire over fame.

LET IT BE YOU.

Let your life interrupt cycles. Let your obedience break curses. Let your purity re-dig ancient wells.

Let your love restore what shame tried to destroy. The earth is groaning. The heavens are watching. The next generation is waiting. And the Father is still asking: *"Whom shall I send?"*

Let the burning man rise. Let him march. Let him carry glory again. The story is not over. It has just begun.

O Lord my God,
By Your mercy and by Your power, I stand now as a
man who chooses fire.

I reject every spirit of passivity, shame, and silent
destruction.

I cast down every idol in my heart.
I tear up every altar of lust, pride, and fear.
I refuse to be a man who survives—I shall be a man
who carries the kingdom.

Every ancestral pattern—break.
Every generational curse—scatter by fire.
Every strange voice in my bloodline—be silenced
now in Jesus' name.

I decree:

I am a son of light.

I am a voice in my generation.

I am a gatekeeper in my family.

I am a priest in my home.

I am a flame on the altar of the Lord.

Let every dormant gift in me come alive.
Let the fire of the Holy Ghost burn through my body,
soul, and spirit.

I will no longer serve God casually.

I will no longer lead in the flesh.

I receive fresh oil.

I receive fresh vision.

I receive divine restoration.

I arise in boldness.

I arise in purity.

I arise in prayer.

I arise in prophetic authority.

Let the sword of the Lord be in my hand.

Let the roar of the Lion be in my mouth.

Let the presence of the Almighty Walk with me.

I will not die in shame.

I will not live in cycles.

I will not be a broken mirror.

I will be a burning man—marked by heaven and feared by hell.

In the name of Jesus Christ,
Amen.

www.ingramcontent.com/pod-product-compliance
Lightning Source LLC
Chambersburg PA
CBHW061431050726

47593CB00006B/2302